LONDON BUSES
1970-1980
A DECADE OF LONDON TRANSPORT
AND LONDON COUNTRY OPERATIONS

LONDON BUSES
1970-1980
A DECADE OF LONDON TRANSPORT
AND LONDON COUNTRY OPERATIONS

PEN & SWORD
TRANSPORT

MATTHEW WHARMBY AND JOHN LAKER

CONTENTS

All photographs in this book were taken by John Laker, the majority with an Agfa Silette camera.

ISBN 978 1 47387 294 3

Published in 2017 by Pen & Sword Transport
an imprint of
Pen & Sword Books Ltd
47 Church Street, Barnsley, South Yorkshire, S70 2AS

Copyright © Matthew Wharmby and John Laker, 2017

Typeset by Matthew Wharmby
Printed and bound by Replika Press Pvt. Ltd.

Pen & Sword Books Ltd incorporates the imprints of Pen & Sword Archaeology, Atlas, Aviation, Battleground, Discovery, Family History, History, Maritime, Military, Naval, Politics, Railways, Select, Transport, True Crime, and Fiction, Frontline Books, Leo Cooper, Praetorian Press, Seaforth Publishing and Wharncliffe.

For a complete list of Pen & Sword titles please contact
PEN & SWORD BOOKS LIMITED
47 Church Street, Barnsley, South Yorkshire, S70 2AS, England
E-mail: enquiries@pen-and-sword.co.uk
Website: www.pen-and-sword.co.uk

Front cover: The old order of classic London buses is exemplified by Harrow Weald's RT 1139, with upper-case blinds throughout.

Back cover, top: The much-loved low-height RLH class bowed out early in the era covered by this book; RLH 59 of Harrow Weald saw out the 230 with them.

Back cover, middle: The green Country Area buses became the property of London Country, but Green Line endured, at first still with modernised RFs like RF 165.

Back cover, bottom: Aldenham continued to overhaul London Transport's buses in the 1970s; this view is of a red Routemaster and a repurchased green RCL coach being treated side by side.

INTRODUCTION

During the decade of the 1970s London's buses were subjected to major changes. The two previous decades had been dominated by the standardised RT and RF fleets in red or green, but the familiar London scene was about to change forever.

From 1 January 1970 London Transport's Country Area buses were hived off to form London Country Bus Services, a subsidiary of the National Bus Company. This involved the transfer of 28 garages and 1,267 vehicles.

The cost of traditional crew operation had come under scrutiny due to falling ridership and staff availability, and a move to one-man operation (OMO) began in 1964, at first using existing RFs. After an experiment which introduced the first Red Arrow route, a fleet of AEC Merlin single-deckers designed for multiple standee flat-fare operation entered service between 1968 and 1970, followed by the shorter Swifts. When double-deck OMO was legalised, new Daimler Fleetlines (DMSs) began to appear in 1971, starting with route 220. These were not successful in London and were not compatible with London Transport's maintenance patterns.

A batch of 164 Scania double-deckers with MCW Metropolitan bodywork were bought in 1975 and were initially crew operated, but a second generation of OMO double-deckers was in the offing, and, in co-operation with British Leyland, the Titan was introduced in 1978 following trials with two prototypes. LT preferred not to be dependent on a single supplier and were pleased when MCW developed the Metrobus as a competitor. The first Metrobuses entered service in 1978 and over 500 had been brought into service by the end of 1980. Leyland National single-deckers replaced some of the Merlins and Swifts from 1976.

In 1977 HM the Queen celebrated 25 years on the throne and the occasion was marked with a fleet of 25 silver-painted Routemasters, temporarily designated SRM. They were launched with a parade at Easter from Hyde Park Corner to Battersea Park via Park Lane, Oxford Street, Regent Street, Whitehall and Westminster Bridge.

In 1979 London celebrated 150 years since the first Omnibus appeared. Again a fleet of Routemasters and one Leyland Fleetline appeared in a commemorative livery, and special events were staged.

1979 saw the end of British Airways' Routemaster operation from the West London Air Terminal to Heathrow, patronage of this service having declined due to the extension of the Piccadilly line to the airport.

This publication is a personal record of the changing 1970s scene, including the later years of the RTs and RFs, a study of the Country Area shortly after the transfer of London Transport's green buses to London Country and the gradual conversion of the route network to one-man operation. Another fascinating feature is a rare look inside Aldenham Works in 1980, when Routemasters were still receiving full overhauls and repaints.

Matthew Wharmby
Walton-on-Thames, December 2016

John Laker
Uxbridge, December 2016

CHAPTER ONE

RTs

Right: What better way to start a section on RTs than with a classic roofbox example? By the time of this account, they were very thin on the ground, especially Saunders ones like RT 1317, photographed at Pett's Hill, Northolt Park on 17 April 1970; indeed, this would have been one of this bus's final appearances.

Right: On 3 January 1969 Twickenham's RT 1765 reposes at the time-honoured but now long-gone Staines stand. Twickenham garage would close on 18 April 1970, passing the 90 (and RT 1765) to Fulwell.

Left: Harrow Weald's RT 4123, in Imperial Drive in South Harrow on 31 January 1970, is carrying upper-case via blinds. This stock number would spend eleven years (1964-75) at Harrow Weald, though after overhaul in December 1968 it was a different combination of chassis and body altogether.

Left: Twickenham-based RT 4183 is caught at the 90B's Yeading stand on Easter Sunday, 30 March 1970. When Twickenham closed three weeks later, this bus would transfer to Norbiton.

Left: Another classic feature of traditional London buses fast disappearing by the time our account starts was upper-case lettering on via blinds; it may have been perceived as harder to read when comparative studies were carried out by London Transport, but it lent buses a gravitas they have never had since. RT 3876 was based at Harrow Weald between April 1967 and April 1972, and this Northwick Park Station capture of 30 May 1969 puts it in front of an RLH, a class which was not to last much longer.

Right: Upper-case via blinds also serve better for short routes, which is what the 297 was when it was introduced on 7 September 1968 as a localisation of the fag end of the old 8, latterly in the person of the 46. On 20 September 1969 RT 4190 at Wembley Stadium is still gleaming from its overhaul four months earlier, and would last at Alperton until May 1971.

Below: RT 2528 spent seven years at Edgware, but this shot of it at Ruislip Manor on 2 May 1970 catches it in its last month here. On 14 June the 114 would be withdrawn between Harrow Weald and Edgware, making it a very short route perfect for SMS OMO four months after that. The library in the background has since been demolished.

Left: In Pinner Road, Northwood Hills we see Hendon's RT 529 on the 183, with full upper-case blinds. This was a period of stability for the route, which was RT-operated on Mondays to Saturdays and RM on Sundays. The former Rex cinema can be seen on the right.

Left: RT 672 heads through Ruislip Manor on its way to Ruislip Lido. This bus is recorded briefly at Harrow Weald between November 1974 and March 1975, but sufficient old blinds from stores still existed to furnish it.

Below: Lisson Grove's pattern of service was most complicated by the 1960s, seeing the 59A on Mondays to Fridays, 159A on Saturdays and 59 on Sundays! The Saturday-only 159A is seen in the hands of Camberwell's RT 3491 on 20 September 1969; it would come off on 13 June 1970.

Above: The forecourt of Harrow Weald garage has long been a good photo pitch; on 23 October 1971 we are rewarded with RTs 1234 and 2622. The 158 was in its last week of operation.

Right: Harrow town centre sees Harrow Weald's RT 1294 during its two and a half years based there.

Left: In Perivale, Bideford Avenue on 16 June 1969 is RT 776, based at Alperton since 1964 and continued in numerical form since another combination of body and chassis was spat out of Aldenham with that fleetnumber in December 1967. The section of the 79A passing under this bridge and onward to Northolt was peak hours only by this time, otherwise having been transferred to new route 297 on 7 September 1968; the 79A itself was one-manned with MBs on 25 October 1969.

Left: Harrow Weald's RT 1588 reposes at Ruislip Lido on 13 June 1970. This was another stock number to remain at the same garage after overhaul, although of course another combination mechanically. The other side of the coin was that some garages liked to get popular chassis back no matter what bonnet number they received at Aldenham.

Left: Southall's RT 1567 is on a shortworking to Perivale when captured on 29 July 1970. It had come to Southall through overhaul in November 1969 and would leave in December 1971. The 105 would stay RT-operated all the way to 1978.

Above: On 31 January 1970 RTs 1713 and 3708 share the forecourt of South Harrow Station's small bus stand. RT 1713 had been outshopped from Aldenham overhaul to Harrow Weald in June 1965 and would leave seven years later; RT 3708, meanwhile, had come to Alperton in December 1969, only for its CoF to expire in October 1972. However, it was recertified to survive until 1977, and for the last thirty years has been the showpiece of the Sydney Bus Museum.

Right: RT 2314 rests in the doorway of Southall garage. It spent a little less than three years here, spanning October 1969 to August 1972.

Left: Harrow Weald's RT 1588 has reached Heathrow Airport on 28 February 1970 after the epic eighteen-mile slog from Mill Hill Broadway. This stock number spent nearly ten years at Harrow Weald, but after overhaul in February 1966 it was a different bus.

Left: On 28 August 1970 RT 2673 heads into town through New Cross. Like RT 1588 above, this stock number actually applied to two buses during its decade at New Cross, this iteration having come of overhaul in November 1967. Although it lasted in service until January 1978, it was not disposed of until late in 1979.

Below: A couple of inches of snow give Ruislip a picture-postcard look on 27 December 1970. Once again, RT 2841 spent nine years (1963-72) based at the one garage (Uxbridge), but the combination of body and chassis was renewed upon overhaul in November 1967. It was withdrawn in September 1972 and sold for scrap.

Right: Hanwell's RT 2879 heads through Yeading on its way to Hayes. It was based at Hanwell from November 1968 to February 1973, but went on to Southall, which ran it until February 1976. It ended its career at Bexleyheath in 1978.

Right: The 209 was converted to MBS OMO on 30 January 1971, but on 24 January 1970 buses like Harrow Weald's RT 2924 at South Harrow station were the staple. It was in its last year, and would leave in November, to be sold to Wombwell Diesels for scrap.

Right: Hendon's RT 3018 is seen in Pinner Road, Northwood. Overhaul had brought it here in January 1968 and it would spend four years working on the 183 until its CoF expired.

Left: On 31 July 1970 Harrow Weald's RT 3109 passes South Harrow Station. It had come to the garage after outshopping from Aldenham overhaul in February 1969 and would stay here until October 1971.

Left: Wembley High Road on 1 August 1970 sees Alperton's RT 3298 passing through on the 83. A number of RTs depicted in this book were stock numbers that worked at one garage despite being overhauled and outshopped as different combinations, but this identity managed to see three separate iterations at Alperton, together working from 1959 until 1973.

Below: Alperton's RT 3325 pulls up to Greenford station on 30 April 1971. This bus spent only three years at Alperton, leaving for Turnham Green in May.

RT 3876 offloads at Rayners Lane in 1970. It was three years into a five-year spell at Harrow Weald, but the 158 would be off its list of routes to work by the end of that term.

Harrow Weald's RT 3386 is seen in Cannon Lane in the bucolic heart of Metroland served by the 209. It served here only two years after overhaul in November 1969, leaving for Abbey Wood in October 1971 and lasting there until 1973.

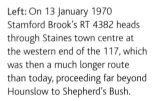

Above: On 4 April 1970 we see RT 4281 at the Vauxhall Bridge Road stand of the 185 just round the corner from Victoria Station. Overhaul had brought it to Walworth garage in December 1968 and it would stay until March 1971.

Left: On 13 January 1970 Stamford Brook's RT 4382 heads through Staines town centre at the western end of the 117, which was then a much longer route than today, proceeding far beyond Hounslow to Shepherd's Bush.

Left: RT 4406 of Uxbridge rests at the 224's station terminus on 3 January 1970. This was the first route of that number in the area, hugging the London border on its west side and proceeding beyond Staines to Laleham, a link no longer even attempted. By this time it fielded just six RTs and would be converted to RF OMO on 16 January 1971. RT 4406 stayed on for another two years before transferring to Middle Row.

Above: The long-established 77 group took passengers down the Wandsworth Road and then off in different directions. This shot at Euston in 1969 shows the two basic routes and their steeds of the time; on the left is Stockwell's RT 4638 and on the right, Merton's RT 4404. Both 77 and 77A were converted to RM on 15 December 1973.

Right: RT 528 of Uxbridge garage waits for the off at Ruislip station on 3 April 1970. It was one of the last RTs to be overhauled, in January, and still looks fine, but it would last here only till the end of the year. A long string of allocations followed until final withdrawal in 1978.

Left: RT 4705 is in Ruislip Road. It came to Southall via overhaul in July 1965 and stayed eight years. After sale in 1976 it made its way to France and was still extant as recently as 2006.

Left: Southall's RT 4466 exits Reservoir Road on the 232. It had been repainted in April 1969, five years into its stint at Southall.

Left: The forecourt of Hounslow bus station on 25 April 1971 sees RT 1357, RM 1099 and SMS 350. The RT was a staff bus and the Swift was one of a number delivered for the 110 and 111 that January.

Right: On 24 January 1970 RT 745 is at Watford Junction. The 292A was a most unlikely weekend route that covered the 292 on Sundays from Borehamwood to Edgware, but then hared off in the other direction, over the 142 in its entirety! The 306 could be taken between Borehamwood and Watford Junction much more directly, and the 292A was pared back to its original length on 13 June. That was when RT 745 left Edgware, but it would last eight more years.

Right: On 16 September 1971 Kingston's RT 1200 finds itself at Leatherhead, at the very southern limit of red bus operation. This bus was five years into a seven-year hitch at Kingston, though neither it nor RT operation on the 71 was under threat at this point.

Left: The junction of Park Road and Uxbridge High Street, with the former Methodist church in the background, is now the site of a major roundabout. RT 2577 was snapped against it on 15 April 1972. This bus would subsequently transfer from Uxbridge to Barking and serve there until February 1978.

Left: On 11 September 1971 Holloway's RT 2712 takes itself down the Kings Road. The 19 was late to go over to RMs, but was in the midst of doing so by the time this photo was taken. It would be the last hurrah for RT 2712, which was sold to Wombwell Diesels in October.

Below: On 18 September 1971 Southall's RT 3240 is heading south from Greenford Broadway. It was withdrawn the following April and sold.

Above: RT 2004 is seen at Ruislip Gardens on 19 December 1970. It had come to Southall from overhaul in August 1966 and would spend five years there before moving on to Catford and finishing its career with North Street.

Right: RT 2523 is at Ruislip Manor not long after repaint and transfer to Harrow Weald in November 1970. It would last here until the end of 1974, by which time the 114 had long been converted to single-deck OMO.

Right: On 7 June 1969 RT 2200 turns at Ruislip Station. This shot puts it right in the middle of its four years spent at Southall, which would prove to be its final operating garage.

Left: The 92A followed the 92 all the way from Southall Garage to Wembley, only diverging at the end to stand at Wembley Stadium, where RT 4705 is seen in the route's dying days; it was withdrawn on 15 May 1971. The bus would stay around rather longer, leaving Southall in September 1973 but lasting another year again due to recertification on a further ticket.

Left and below: Two portrayals of Harrow Weald's RT 817; left passing along Ruislip High Street on 10 September 1971, and below in Lascelles Avenue between Harrow and South Harrow on the 158, a Reshaping casualty that came off on 30 October 1971, taking RT 817 with it.

Right: RT 3284 has arrived at Ruislip station in this shot. Overhaul had brought it to Southall in January 1969 and it would spend the next four years there; its final garage was Catford, from where it was withdrawn in May 1978.

Above: The 273 had been a creation of the Ealing-area Reshaping conversions, but on 17 June 1972 it was projected from Ruislip over the withdrawn 98A to Hayes. That brought Southall buses to Ickenham, where RT 3392 is seen on 15 September. This bus had come to Southall in February and would last just twelve more months before withdrawal.

Right: RT 3947 is seen at Greenford on 30 April 1971. It had been outshopped from overhaul to Alperton in November 1966, but this would be its last year in service and it was withdrawn in October.

Above: It's cold enough on 23 February 1971 for Norbiton's RT 990 to require some cardboard over the radiator grille, to seal in the heat. After 1968 the section of the 65 beyond Ealing Broadway to Argyle Road was peak hours only. Norbiton was RT 990's last garage in service, but after August 1975 it went on to staff bus use until 1978.

Left: RT 1294 is seen passing along Lower Road in Roxeth. It served at Harrow Weald between April 1970 and November 1972, but saw further use after the latter date, working out of Shepherd's Bush and North Street before being turned into a trainer, in which role it lasted until 1977.

Above: RT 1353 is at the Northwood Station terminus of the 183 on 6 November 1971. Its transfer to Hendon had accompanied repainting in October 1970, and it would spend the next four years there.

Right: RT 1376 spent only nine months at Uxbridge, from July 1971 to April 1972, but during that period worked on the 98, whose eastern terminus was Hounslow bus station.

Above: RT 1376 is seen again during its short spell at Uxbridge, this time on 2 June 1972 on the 98A, the second of three routes to bear that number and in this case lasting only four years. It would be withdrawn on the 17th.

Below: RTs on the 207 were a great rarity, but on 26 February 1972 Uxbridge put out RT 1648. There are certainly more via points available to the passengers boarding than on the comparable RML. RT 1648 spent from February to November 1972 at Uxbridge but continued to wander, serving at four more garages before withdrawal in October 1976.

Above: RT 2554 rests at Hillingdon Station on 15 April 1972. This woud be the last spring of RTs on the 98, as SMSs would come on 6 January of the following year, but RT 2554 had already gone by then; it moved to Southall in June.

Right: RT 3319 is is Ruislip Road, Yeading, on 14 July 1972. It was withdrawn shortly afterwards and sold by the end of the year.

Above: Southall's RT 3284 is loading up at Ruislip on 17 July 1971. It would leave this garage at the end of 1972 but would last all the way to 1978.

Left: RT 3876 passes Northolt Park station on 4 September 1971. This bus would last at Harrow Weald until April 1972.

Below: Harrow Weald's RT 3812 turns from Reservoir Road into Bury Street on 29 August 1970. The blinds are in a confused state, with a canopy blind in the front box and a rear blind in the side box! Originally a green stock number, RT 3812 had come to Harrow Weald from overhaul in November 1965 and would spend seven years here.

Above: RT 3851 is at Hillingdon Heath on 2 June 1972. For such a long route, the 98 had a very low peak vehicle requirement (PVR) at the time, just five RTs on Mondays to Fridays, but then again the 98A accounted for the rest. This bus left Uxbridge in November but was later recertified – three times, in fact – and lasted until 1975.

Right: RT 4009's lights blaze outside Ruislip Station one evening in the early 1970s. It had come to Uxbridge from overhaul in April 1967 and stayed until April 1972, being sold for scrap at the end of that year.

Above: RTs galore at Northolt station. RT 2655, heading towards the camera, served at Harrow Weald between February 1968 and February 1973.

Left: The second 98A took the middle portion of the main route via Judge Heath Lane and Botwell Lane rather than the Uxbridge Road, and terminated at Hatton Cross. It is seen in the form of RT 2739 at Ruislip Station on 9 June 1972, in its last week of operation. RT 2739 had only come to Uxbridge in January and would leave after the 98A came off, passing to Harrow Weald.

Left: Norbiton would be the last operational garage of RT 365 after a long career spanning more than a dozen garages. On 8 June 1972 it is loading at Ealing Broadway.

Above: RT 4282 is seen in Shaftesbury Avenue, Harrow. It had come to Harrow Weald through overhaul in November 1969 and would stay until October 1974, after which it was sold to Wombwell Diesels.

Right: Southall's RT 4329 passes Park Royal station on 26 July 1973. It would leave the garage at the end of the year, but go on to serve at Alperton, Willesden, Riverside and Harrow Weald before sale in October 1977.

Left: Southall's RT 3392 heads along Ruislip Road on 2 June 1972. It had been transferred from Fulwell three months earlier, taking up a second spell at Southall after an earlier prolonged period spanning 1963-68. It was withdrawn in February 1973 and sold.

Left: RT 3470 traverses the Greenford roundabout on 28 October 1972. It had come to Southall after overhaul in July 1968, but the five-year ticket bestowed at that point expired in July 1973 and further service depended on recertification. It got it, and lasted until 1976, albeit for much of that time as a trainer or in store.

Left: On 16 May 1970 RT 4152 heads for Ruislip along West End Road, passing Grosvenor Vale, at the tail end of its six-year spell at Southall (which spanned an overhaul); in August it would undergo a repaint and then transfer to Elmers End.

Right: On 1 May 1971 Southall's RT 4110 rounds the roundabout at Greenford, heading for Wembley. A green bus for its first eighteen years, it came to Southall ex-overhaul in February 1969; when the 273 was one-manned on 6 January 1973 it departed for Upton Park and would survive until 1976, its final garage being Sutton.

Above: It's cold and misty at Hillingdon on New Year's Day 1973, but not so much so as to leave the camera at home. In any case, there are only five days left of RTs on the 273, so it's incumbent on photographers to capture as many as they can, lest books like this become a possibility in forty years! RT 4128 stayed at Southall anyway.

Right: RT 4699 pulls out to overtake RT 4329 at Hayes & Harlington Station on 1 May 1971. The former would leave for Harrow Weald in January 1973 when the 98 was one-manned, while the latter's fate is explored on the opposite page.

Left: RT 4329 heads down Ruislip High Street on the last leg of its journey from Hounslow. It was based at Uxbridge between November 1968 and June 1971, but survived to work out of four more garages until 1977.

Left: The 1 has somehow never lived up to its expectations for what one would think would be a flagship route number; instead, it's crept round the back of the major tourist points and had both its outer termini hacked off without pity. Similarly, it was not seen fit to convert it to anything more modern than RTs until 1975. On 12 December 1972 New Cross's RT 4448 sets off from Marylebone; this was its second spell at New Cross, but even after the conversion of the 1 to RM it would bounce around further south-east London sheds before final withdrawal from Catford in June 1978.

Left: RT 486 of Southall garage is crossing Greenford Broadway on 18 September 1971. This bus would have an unusually stable later life, having come to Southall from overhaul in September 1967 and staying until November 1976.

Above: Tram replacement route 109, introduced in 1951 to take over tram routes 16 and 18 and expanding to cover more than the trams could, was so heavily provisioned that it took until 1976 before RMs replaced its RTs at Brixton and Thornton Heath. Originally a Country Area green bus, RT 4166, seen in the company of Obsolete Fleet ST 922, left Brixton in September 1976, but stuck around until 1978, sometimes as a trainer, sometimes recertified for further service.

Right: 28 December 1974 and the 183 has a week left of RT operation before DMSs take over on 4 January 1975. Hendon's RT 2654, seen at Pinner, left for Kingston where it would enjoy another eighteen months of service.

Left: On 19 August 1973 RTs 1798 and 1184 rest in the doorways of their home garage, Southall. The 120 would succumb to OMO DMS on 28 January 1978 and RMs would take over the 105 on 30 April of the same year. RT 1798 sidestepped withdrawal at this point and lasted all the way to the end at Barking, which has ensured its preserved status today, while RT 1184 was not so lucky, coming off in June 1977, even before the 120's one-manning.

Left: RT 4773 presides over a gathering of its route 140 colleagues inside Harrow Weald garage. This bus, for the first fifteen years of its life a green stock number, came into the red bus fold after overhaul in 1969 and served at Holloway (both of them) until transferring to Harrow Weald in August 1975. However, it didn't last until the end of RTs on the 140 and was withdrawn in January 1977, to be sold in March for scrap.

Left: RT 1599 was the class's representative at the Silver Jubilee parade on 10 April 1977 and was repainted for the purpose. After that it would go into service at Harrow Weald and see out the class there on the 140 on 15 July 1978. It is preserved today.

Above: Almost the end for the RT. After the conversion of the 87 to RM on 28 October 1978, just the unassuming 62 was left, operated by thirteen Barking RTs. Two of them, RTs 3016 and 4633, are captured at the route's Barkingside terminus on 3 February 1979. The last day would be 7 April, carried out in front of huge crowds.

Right: After 7 April 1979, the only examples of the RT family to be seen in London were in the hands of preservationists; RTW 29 at Battersea Park on the 15th is accompanied by a similarly vanished symbol of London, a family of Pearly Kings and Queens.

Left: After the disposal of the last RT trainers and staff buses at the end of 1979, the number actually held in stock by London Transport fell to single figures. RT 2143 was retained as the Skid Bus on the famous patch at Chiswick and is seen there on 4 March 1980. The RT with this stock number had been new to Uxbridge in 1949.

Left and below: RT 113 is in splendid full wartime garb when sighted at Chiswick on 1 May 1980; all that it needs are the mesh window coverings to ward against splintered glass from bomb blast, and there's rather less risk of that sort of thing happening to it, even in certain parts of London in the late 1970s and early 1980s! Although the batch of 150 from which it came are commonly termed 'pre-war' RTs, the war was already under way by the time they started entering service.

CHAPTER TWO

RFs

Right: Although most OMO conversions in the era covered by this book were carried out by Merlins and Swifts, the large number of RFs remaining played their part. The 223 at Uxbridge was converted from RT to RF on 16 January 1971 and on 30 July we see RF 338, fresh out of overhaul, at Ruislip.

Below: RF 338 is seen again, this time at Ickenham. The 223 upon one-manning had been handed the responsibility of taking passengers to Heathrow and RFs (including RF 338) would last on it until 1976, when DMSs took over.

Left: RF 360 was another example put into Uxbridge after overhaul in August 1971. It is seen in Uxbridge, opposite St Andrew's Church and would last here until May 1976.

Below: On 11 July 1971 RF 346 swings into Ruislip High Street on the last leg of its journey to Ruislip Station. This RF was only based at Uxbridge from January to December of 1971, leaving for overhaul and thence to Kingston.

Above: Pulling into Ruislip Station forecourt and about to make the swing through one hundred and eighty degrees to the 223's first stop is RF 349. This was its second innings at Uxbridge, a previous spell having taken in 1959-61. In spite of an overhaul it would leave in June 1973 but return in September to finish off the last three years of its career.

Right: On 16 June 1972 Uxbridge's RF 407 passes along Botwell Lane in Hayes, the sole responsibility of the 204. This route had exchanged RTs for RFs on 16 January 1971 and would further convert to SMSs on 30 June 1973.

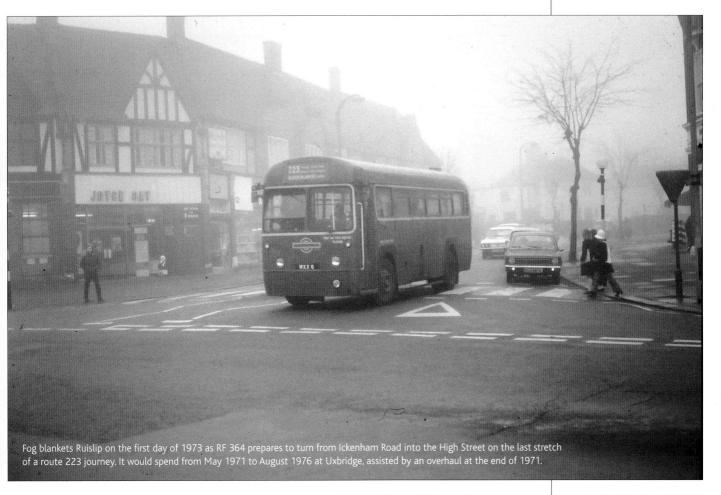

Fog blankets Ruislip on the first day of 1973 as RF 364 prepares to turn from Ickenham Road into the High Street on the last stretch of a route 223 journey. It would spend from May 1971 to August 1976 at Uxbridge, assisted by an overhaul at the end of 1971.

RF 396 prepares to make the right turn into Uxbridge station forecourt during 1971. It had come to Uxbridge in January but would depart in November for overhaul. At the very end of its life, however, it would return to Uxbridge in March 1976 for a few last months. The 224 picked round the western fringes of the GLC area and was one-manned on 16 January 1971.

Right: RF 418 picks up at West Ruislip Station. It had come to Uxbridge as part of a large contingent intended to convert the 204, 223, 224 and 224B to OMO on 16 January 1971, but this one would depart upon overhaul in December.

Right: RF 340 was outshopped to Uxbridge following overhaul in August 1971 and is seen in the town centre shortly after. It would last here until June 1973. Following pedestrianisation, buses no longer run through here.

Right: On 16 July 1972 Uxbridge's RF 406 has reached Uxbridge Station. It's six months out of overhaul and still looks fresh; it would serve another four years at Uxbridge before withdrawal. After post-London Transport use as a school bus, it would enter the ranks of preserved RFs and can still be enjoyed today.

Left: At the front of Uxbridge station, long before this part of the town centre was pedestrianised, RF 598 loads up on 26 February 1972, working only as far as West Drayton. It was just out of overhaul and would stay until July 1976.

Left: RF 598 is seen again, this time In Belmont Road about to turn into Bakers Road, at the end of which sits Uxbridge station.

Below: This stabling point at Uxbridge station yard is seen packed four across with RFs. From left to right are RFs 364, 402, 345 and 324. The present garage was built on this site.

Right: On 24 January 1970 Harrow Weald's RF 421 is seen in College Road. It had arrived in July 1966 when the 136 was introduced and would leave after 24 July 1971 when MBSs took over. It can be seen in active preservation today.

Below: Kingston's 218 and 219 were the final two RF routes, but RF 424 wouldn't be there at the finish in 1979; on 13 May 1969 it is at the old Staines stand with Addlestone's RLH 44 beside it.

Above: Harrow Weald's RF 315 pulls onto the 136's stop at South Harrow Station in 1970. Despite being from a red batch, it spent a great deal of its modern preservation era in green.

Left: Kingston's RF 319 is seen at Staines on 3 January 1970. Kingston would be its last garage, and after March 1976 it was sold, subsequently passing through the hands of various preservationists and still to be seen on the circuit today. The 218 was converted to LS after the RF era and then dropped out of the London bus network altogether, to be reborn under numerous identities (one of which was 218!) with myriad private companies.

Right: On 26 September 1976 Edgware's RF 685 reposes at its home garage alongside a DMS. A Country Area green bus for its first fifteen and a half years, it would go into red in 1969 and hop from garage to garage thereafter; even Edgware was only a thirteen-month deployment and it would finish at Kingston.

Below: On 22 May 1970 Harrow Weald's RF 421 passes the unmistakable facade of Harrow School. This bus had been based at Harrow Weald for four years, but would transfer out to Uxbridge at the end of 1971; even so, five more years remained for it, including an overhaul in 1973.

Above: RF 324 has reached the end of Judge Heath Lane on 2 June 1972, at the halfway mark of RF operation on the 204. It would leave for Kingston the following June, when the 204 went over to SMS.

Left: The 285 was RM-operated on Mondays to Saturdays, but on Sundays between 19 July 1969 and 27 March 1971 both Hounslow and Norbiton used RFs. RF 333, seen departing Kingston station on 30 March 1970, belonged to the latter. It would finish its career at Edgware.

Above and below: On 16 March 1972 Edgware's RF 512 finds itself with its radiator cap cover undone and the inspector at Stanmore perhaps less interested in remedying it than he should be. The filler was ingeniously covered by the roundel device, a piece of sensible engineering that has also made the blind box openable from the outside, unlike on modern buses where all sorts of impediments get in the way of the blinds. After seeing out the 218 and 219 at Kingston RF 512 entered preservation.

Left: On 21 August 1976 Uxbridge's RF 537 finds itself at West Drayton Station, with RF 505 a hundred yards behind it. In four months' time the 223 will gain an upper deck when DMSs take over, and SMSs will similarly displace RFs from the 224. This wouldn't be the end for either bus, however; not just yet. RF 537 would be transferred to Kingston and RF 505 to Hounslow.

Below: RFs duly made their gala finish on 31 March 1979 and thereafter the only representatives were preserved. Among their number was RF 10, one of the twenty-five private-hire examples taken in 1951 to kick off the class, and distinguishable by their short length and roof windows. It is seen at the Hyde Park Easter parade on 15 April 1979.

CHAPTER THREE

RLHs

Above: There were only four RLH-operated routes in the Central Area by the time of our account, and one was the 230 out of Harrow Weald. It was replaced by flat-fare MBS-operated H1 on 14 June 1969. The low bridge in Headstone Drive under the West Coast Main Line necessitated low-height buses, one of which is RLH 63 on 30 November 1968.

Right: At the North Harrow end of the short 230 we see RLH 57 on 19 May 1969. There was no provision for a rear route number box on the RLH, which had been bought off-the-peg as a standard manufacturer's product but was nonetheless treated with considerable regard. RLH 57 went on to Dalston to see out the class on the 178.

Left: With lights ablaze, Harrow Weald's RLH stands at Rayners Lane on the evening of 28 January 1969. This bus had had an eventful life, being transferred around the RLH operators and even after the 230 was lost to the type, would go on to Hornchurch to see out its career on the 248 and 248A.

Left: Harrow Weald's final complement comprised RLHs 27, 57, 59, 60, 62, 63, 68 and 74, but RLH 27 was the only green one. After a decade at Addlestone and then to Reigate, it had come to Harrow Weald in September 1968 without the benefit of a repaint, and is seen at Rayners Lane on 19 May 1969.

Above: RLH 27 again, the only green representative at Harrow Weald. On 30 November 1968 it is passing under the Headstone Drive bridge.

Right: There was at least some provision on the RLH for the passenger approaching from the rear, and it was to the same size as the simple front blinds. The 230 was short enough, in fact, to need just a lazy blind with only the two termini displayed; in truth, you could walk between the two and not have too remote a prospect of catching the bus up! This shot of RLH 27 was taken at Rayners Lane on 19 May 1969.

Left: RLH 57 is at Rayners Lane on 19 May 1969; withdrawal and replacement by the H1 was but weeks away, obliging photographers to get their shots in.

Left: RLH 60 is in Imperial Drive on 19 May 1969. This bus would be withdrawn after the 230 came off, with no further allocations. It departed for California and is still there.

Left: Metroland mock-Tudor is in evidence in Parkside Way as RLH 59 plies the 230 on its last day, 13 June 1969. This was also exported to the USA after withdrawal but only made it there in parts form.

Right: RLH 60 coasts along Imperial Drive on 19 May 1969. The 230 had these roads generally north and west of Harrow town centre to itself, forming a loose semi-circle around it that was not added to when the H1 took its place, though plans had existed to bring the southern end into Harrow proper. Subsequent iterations have turned it into a circular, numbered variously 201 and 211 and today going under H9 and H10.

Right: On the same day, RLH 62 has completed another journey to Rayners Lane and decants its passengers. It was not seen fit to equip the RLHs with specifically nearside rear turn signal indicators in the manner of the RTs, though twin reflectors did manage to make it to RLH backs under legislation. RLH 62 also made it to the States; a large number did at this time, thanks to the generally lower heights of bridges and lamp-posts in the USA.

Right: And at the other end of the 230, RLH 74 comes up alongside fellow Harrow Weald RT 3876 on 30 May 1969. RLH 74 was yet another to cross the pond, though in this case to Atlanta, Georgia rather than California.

Coming up to Rayners Lane on 19 May 1969 is RLH 62. After sale by London Transport it spent 38 years in Columbus, Ohio before a subsequent purchaser took it further east.

Kenton is where RLH 68 is seen on 13 June 1969. Although it escaped withdrawal at this point and served one last year at Hornchurch, another U.S. state beckoned after sale, to add to the variety of American locations that had taken to the RLH. This was Virginia, where RLH 68 was used by the City of Hampton to take passengers on tours of Langley Air Force Base.

CHAPTER FOUR

London Country

Right: When London Country took over the green buses of London Transport on 1 January 1970, it inherited a small number of GSs; some lasted in service on Garston's 336A to Loudwater Village until 30 March 1972, while the rest were trainers. GS 55 belonged to Reigate in this capacity and is seen having journeyed to Leatherhead garage on 16 September 1971.

Right: A similar small class that was expected to go sooner rather than later once inherited by London Country was the RLH. Twelve of the seventeen that came across belonged to Addlestone and the others to Guildford, and on 27 March 1970 the latter's RLH 13 is seen at the 436's Staines stand. It was withdrawn with the rest in July and eventually made its way to the Netherlands.

Left: On 14 February 1970 Amersham's RT 3315 sets off from High Wycombe garage on the 362. Although the majority of the 484 RTs inherited by London Country had come off by 1972, this one lingered until 1976, finishing its career at Harlow.

Left: On the same day RT 3315 is seen again at High Wycombe station.

Left: Staines operated RT services on the south-west finges of London as London Transport gave way to London Country, and on 3 January 1970 RT 3420 passes through the town centre on the way to the bridge. The 441 group was not one-manned until 1977, but RT 3420 was an early withdrawal, falling out in January 1972 with CoF expiry.

Right: Windsor's RT 3657 sets off from Uxbridge for Windsor on 11 July 1970. It was repainted in November but lasted only another fifteen months in service.

Right: Amersham garage plays host to RT 4511 on 28 January 1970; the new order is nowhere in evidence on any of bus, garage or signage. The 353 was converted to OMO with SMs on 20 February 1971, obliging RT 4511 to leave; it survived at Swanley and then Stevenage until the end of 1972.

Right: The other aspect of Amersham garage on 28 January 1970, again with RT 4511 in attendance.

Left: This 27 March 1970 shot of Addlestone garage's forecourt sees all of RT, RF and RLH represented; despite having been transferred here only as recently as June 1968, RT 4749 would work from no further garages after this and was withdrawn in April 1971.

Left: Still in Green Line livery and looking smart for it despite having been demoted to bus work since the arrival of coach-seated Routemasters, Windsor's RT 605 is captured at Cippenham on 20 February 1970. It was repainted in December but lasted only until February 1972.

Left: A peep into Amersham's entrance in the early days of London Country gives us RTs 3249 and 600. The former was transferred to Hemel Hempstead in March 1970 and withdrawn in June 1972, while RT 600 didn't even last that long, coming out of service in June 1970.

Right: The sheer elegance of the RT's swept-back profile persisted to the end, no matter how dishevelled the vehicles became under London Country ownership. RT 4045 of Amersham is seen at Windsor bus station on 3 January 1970. It was very much a dilettante where transfers were concerned, moving on to Stevenage before this month was through and seeing further use at Chelsham until its passenger-carrying life came to an end in August 1974.

Right: Garston's RT 3576 is taking the 321 road through Denham on 7 February 1970. This woud be its last deployment; even before Atlanteans came to the 321, it was withdrawn in March 1972 and sold for scrap.

Right: RT 4100 prepares to leave Uxbridge on the 457A on 13 February 1970. It had been a fixture at Windsor since 1963, an overhaul in March 1968 returning another combination of chassis and body under that fleetnumber, but in April 1971 it left for Swanley and would end its career at Stevenage in June 1972.

Left: By the last day of 1970, new LONDON COUNTRY signage has been applied to the front of Amersham garage, propped up by RTs 3172 and 1008. Neither had long left, the former being withdrawn in February 1971 and the latter in January.

Left: It's still cold enough on 14 February 1970 for High Wycombe's engineers to have had to help out RT 4112 with a piece of cardboard locking the heat into its radiator. Seen at High Wycombe Police Station, it had three years left, but at various garages, specifically Tring, High Wycombe (again), Godstone, Chelsham and Garston.

Left: The addition of a yellow band to London Country's inherited Lincoln green in replacement of latter-1960s flake grey really brought the colour out in the company's ageing buses. RT 4495 was a Garston motor when captured at Uxbridge on 26 February 1972, but had only been here since the previous August and would be off again in July, to gallivant round a series of garages (Leatherhead, Reigate, Dorking, Staines, Dorking (again), Staines (again), Guildford and finally Staines (yet again) before sale for scrap in September 1976.

Right: RT 4511 is seen in Amersham on 28 January 1970; it had been based here since June 1968 and would move on in March 1971.

Right: RT 4741 is in Luton on 14 March 1970, operating that garage's short 360. RTs would linger here until 1976, but this bus wasn't one of them; it was withdrawn in July 1971.

Left: On 20 February 1970 Windsor's RT 4766 is seen in Windsor Road, Slough. The pace of change to the route structure since London Transport has been bewildering even to enthusiasts, but the 441 is at least partially recognisable today. This bus was withdrawn in October 1972.

Left: The 385 group was one-manned on 15 July 1972, but on 24 January 1970 Garston's RT 4761 is in charge at Watford Junction. It wouldn't survive long enough to see its routes lost, coming off in July 1971.

Left: Windsor's RT 979 looks resplendent in Green Line livery as the sun sets over Slough on 3 January 1970, but its coaching days are long behind. The 446 group succumbed to OMO on 14 October 1972, but RT 979 came off long before that, in February of that year.

Above: The RT's classic offside profile, but enlivened by the addition of London Country's shortlived but likeable logo. RT 987 belonged to Windsor and this shot places it in Uxbridge during 1970. It was lucky enough to go for overhaul at the end of 1971, which bought it five more years in service.

Right: Also at Uxbridge, but on 11 September 1971, RTs 987 and 3867 share the station approach road. RT 3867 lasted until April 1972.

Right: RT 3898 is in Luton on 14 March 1970. It had come to Garston ex-overhaul in December 1968 and would pass to London Country on 1 January 1970. Following the conversion of the 321 to AN OMO it would head on to Hemel Hempstead.

Left: At the gateway of Amersham garage (albeit no longer London Transport) on 18 February 1970 is RT 2785, just having been brought in by a learner driver. It didn't stay long here, only from December 1969 to June 1970, but that was long enough to cement it with London Country.

Left: Windsor garage on 3 January 1970 sees RTs 3899, 3118 and 979. RT 3899 had been based here since December 1968 and would leave in February 1972; RT 3118 (or at least the bonnet number, which had shared two post-overhaul combinations) spent from October 1961 to April 1971 at Windsor before lasting five more years at Hemel Hempstead and Garston, and RT 979 worked here only until February 1972, after which it was sold.

Left: RT 987 circumnavigates Uxbridge town centre during 1970. It had only come to Windsor in January and would depart again before long, in this case via overhaul.

Right: As well as 484 RTs, London Country inherited 413 RFs. The RFs had a little more time left in them than the RTs, especially the refurbished Green Line examples, but more than enough were downgraded service buses like RF 226, seen at Crawley garage on 27 March 1970 in the hands of East Grinstead garage. It survived until December 1975, latterly at Leatherhead, and is in preservation today.

Right: Dorking's RF 249 was another Green Line coach downgraded to bus work, and on 23 March 1970 at Dorking, has had its LONDON TRANSPORT fleetnames removed and primer applied ready for the new ones. It was withdrawn from Hertford garage in December 1973 but not sold until 1975.

Right: Uniquely for the era, the registrations of most of the dedicated Country Area bus RFs matched their fleetnumbers. RF 541, new in April 1953, was at Windsor by the time the changeover to London Country came, and on 3 January 1970 is seen in Uxbridge. It finished its days at Guildford in December 1972 and was sold for scrap.

Above: Dorking garage plays host to five RFs on 27 March 1970, namely RFs 271, 675, 374, 593 and 42, but it's the red one, RF 374, that's of particular interest as it was on a long-term loan that ultimately spanned the changeover to London Country. It spent the period from October 1969 to March 1971 here and then returned to its parent for sale and ultimate scrapping.

Left: On 14 February 1970 High Wycombe's RF 670 is seen on the 442 at High Wycombe Police Station; the blinds are full of via points but without a destination! It would subsequently work out of Amersham and Hemel Hempstead before withdrawal in May 1975.

The registration numbers on these RFs would mark them out as near-siblings, but don't be deceived; these are actually RFs 307 and 295, which gained their new identities (ex-RFs 526 and 514) when a complicated swap was executed in 1957 to align several Green Line conversions with one another. Seen on 28 January 1970 at Amersham, their mutual home by then, they lasted (as buses) until 1975 and 1973 respectively.

RF 700, the highest-numbered and last of the RFs, in Hill End Road, Harefield on 7 February 1970. Garston would be its final garage, and it would finish there in February 1973.

Left and below left: On the afternoon of 29 July 1973 Windsor's RF 458 takes on its first passenger at Uxbridge. Although the bus's London Transport legend has been removed from the roundel-shaped radiator cap cover, it has been enlivened with yellow window surrounds, which worked so well over Lincoln green. This bus had arrived at Windsor the previous December and would stay until February 1976.

Below: Based at Leatherhead since the end of 1958, RF 637 was another long-established dedicated Country Area bus and passed on 1 January 1970 to London Country with 412 other RFs. On 27 March it is seen passing Reigate garage, with three years left to go.

Above: On 27 March 1970 Green Line RF 144 passes through Reigate on the 711. There were 150 modernised RFs, which were preferred over newer purchases due to the unreliability of the coach chassis available at the time. RF 144 had been modernised in 1967 and by the time of this photo was based at High Wycombe, though as its career continued it would later work from St Albans, Swanley and finally Northfleet.

Right: Windsor garage on 20 February 1970 sees RF 114 and RMC 1479. The RF was transferred to Staines as a common bus in March 1972 and spent its last year there.

Left: At High Wycombe garage on 14 February 1970, RF 141 still has a Green Line roundel but RF 34 doesn't. Neither vehicle survives today, RF 141 having been scrapped in 1975 and RF 34 in 1978, but the registration of RF 141 lives on, now on preserved RF 202!

Below: High Wycombe garage on 1 February 1970 plays host to two modernised Green Line RFs, one of which is RF 105. This was seven months into a posting which would last until July 1973.

Left: This is Staines garage, seen on 3 January 1970 with an RT and RF 214 visible. The RF had been here since December 1966; it would stay long enough for a repaint (April 1971) and then leave in December 1972, to serve nearly five more years at Windsor.

Amersham's RF 165 takes advantage of the hospitality of London Transport's Uxbridge bus station on 16 July 1972; it has had a 'flying Polo' symbol applied where the Green Line roundel would have been, and looks good for it. Three months later, upon transfer to Stevenage, it would take up a new and less glamorous role as a plain bus, lasting there until January 1975.

RF 82 comes up to Hillingdon Heath in the spring of 1972, heading for High Wycombe via Uxbridge. Shortly after this photo was taken it was transferred from High Wycombe to Staines.

Left: On 3 January 1970 RF 120 finds itself at Windsor bus station, at the tail end of the 725's long slog across south London. It had been at Dartford for this task since March 1969 and would undergo an overhaul at the end of 1970 to enable it to continue, but demotion to bus work was its inevitable lot, as was that of all coach RFs, and that meant transfer away in March 1972, to Dunton Green. Several more transfers were to follow, but it came to the end of the line at Windsor in April 1977.

Left: Swanley's RF 128 is wearing outsize transfers by comparison with the small gold ones historically carried by the modernised variant of the RF class. In this shot it is at Wrotham, preparing for the long haul clear across London and out the other side, to Hemel Hempstead, a journey that would never be imaginable today thanks to traffic, which indeed doomed all the Green Line routes sooner or later. .

Left: St George's Church is the centrepiece of Wrotham, and plays host on 28 March 1973 to an equally elegant and timeless form of transport in the shape of RF 128. It spent from October 1969 to December 1973 at Swanley and was then withdrawn.

Above: High Wycombe's' RF 145 rests outside Reigate garage on 27 March 1970. When the RC class took over the 711 on 18 October this vehicle moved to St Albans and lasted three and a half years there; its final eighteen months were spent at Hemel Hempstead.

Right: At Staines on 28 February 1970 is Northfleet's RF 213, come all the way from Gravesend on the 701. Three years later it would be downgraded to bus mode, repainted for the purpose and returned to service at Leatherhead, with a spell at Addlestone. It is one of the number able to be seen in preservation today.

Right: Snow covers Gerrards Cross on 14 February 1970 as RF 181 happens through. It had just been put into Reigate, but would last only until September before moving on to Windsor, but its final five years of life were characterised by further moves which took it to Staines and finally Chelsham.

Left: High Wycombe's RF 185 is blinded for the 711 as it reposes outside its home garage on the first day of February 1970. Modernisation in May 1967 had brought it here and it would stay until March 1973, though further work beckoned until it was withdrawn in January 1977 and scrapped later that year.

Below: Amersham's RF 172 is seen in the Uxbridge Road heading for town as its tenure as a dedicated Green Line coach winds down; between October 1972 and its withdrawal in December 1973 it would function as a plain bus.

The modernised Green Line RFs wore their London Country green band well. RF 26 was numerically the first, new back in October 1951, and by the time of the sale to LCBS was still engaged upon this prestige work, spending all of 1969 and half of 1970 based at Dorking for the 714. Seen at Luton, it later passed into preservation and can be enjoyed today.

Coming up to Amersham garage is Green Line RF 172, modernised at the end of 1966 and seen on 28 January 1970. It spent 1963-73 at Amersham, after which it moved to High Wycombe before delicensing in December 1973.

Left and below left: RF profiles in London Transport Country Area Lincoln green and drab NBC leaf green without relief. RF 615 of Reigate is seen at Dorking on 27 March 1970, while RF 559 belonged to Windsor when snapped at Wexham Hospital on 7 April 1974.

Below: The RMC class of Green Line coaches was downgraded to bus work as time went on, and during 1976 RMC 1457 is seen at Uxbridge. It had come from Dartford at the end of the previous year and would leave for Chelsham in March 1978, even before the 347 was one-manned and the 347A renumbered 348. After that, it returned to London Transport and spent the 1980s as a trainer.

Above: RMLs 2306-2355 and 2411-2460 were new as green buses. On 7 February 1970 at Harefield Village Garston's RML 2320 hasn't yet received LONDON COUNTRY fleetnames.

Below: By 1973 RML 2457, working from Windsor and sighted at Uxbridge, had received the fleetnames but not the yellow band; it would be overhauled at the end of the year.

Above: Windsor's RML 2436 passes its home garage on 20 February 1970. It served at nowhere else and was scrapped before it could make it back to London Transport.

Below: Red and green on Christmas Eve 1972 as RML 2440 from Garston passes the old Uxbridge garage, where some of its old colleagues still reside.

Right: RML 2428 is ushering out the London Transport era when captured at Northwood on 24 August 1969. It was new to Garston in March 1966 and stayed there for most of its career as a green bus, following which it was taken back by LT and operated until 2004.

Right: Hemel Hempstead was operating RML 2414 by the time this shot was taken at Uxbridge on 16 February 1972, and it looks smart caught between the gold-leaf fleetnumber era of London Transport and the promising early beginnings of London Country, with its yellow band and flying Polo logo.

Right: The NBC leaf green livery applied to London Country vehicles from the mid-1970s was far from lovely, but the RMLs wore it as well as might be expected. On 24 February 1973 Garston's RML 2420 reposes at Uxbridge, with a much smarter MCW-bodied AN 107 behind. This was one of the small number of Routemasters not to make it back to London Transport service; it was scrapped at the beginning of 1978.

Left: Anxious to modernise the Green Line image while shoring it up with RCLs, London Transport ordered fourteen AEC Reliances with Willowbrook bodies and put them into service at the end of 1965. However, they suffered from extreme mechanical unreliability and the avant-garde livery they wore when new didn't help. Repaint and redeployment followed, and on 10 February 1971 RC 12 finds itself at Beaconsfield, based at High Wycombe for the 711. Like the others (barring one fire casualty), it was eventually demoted to bus work and sold for scrap. None survive today.

Below: One of the first orders of business once the new London Country got under way was to continue modernising the Green Line network with increased OMO. Ninety Plaxton-bodied AEC Reliances were ordered, arriving in the first quarter of 1972 as the RP class. RP 32 was later allocated to Staines and is seen at Uxbridge on 29 July 1973.

Right: MBs 81-113 were new as green Country Area buses and passed to London Country. They were dual-door conventional OMO buses but with the much-disliked low driving position. MB 98 spent most of its career at High Wycombe, and is seen in Beaconsfield on 10 February 1971, bearing not just the new fleetname but the new 'flying Polo' logo of the first months of London Country.

Right: MB 113 was the last of the green dual-door MBs and was allocated new to Crawley, where it is seen in 1970. The London Transport roundel has gone from the front, but with nothing yet in replacement. MB 113 would be transferred to Garston at the end of the year and spent the rest of its career there.

Right: New to Garston and destined to spend all ten years (1969-79) of its career there, MB 105 tackles wintry conditions in Gerrards Cross on 14 February 1970. There is damage to the front wing, caused by the lower profile of Merlins by comparison with their predecessors.

Left: Garston's MBS 277 is in a half-and-half state when captured in Prestwick Road, Oxhey on 7 February 1970; the London Transport roundel is still there, but there's a new LONDON COUNTRY fleetname on the side. MBSs 270-303 and 398-438 formed the flat-fare OMO proportion of Merlin allocations to the Country Area and passed to London Country. This particular bus would last until 1979, when it was sold to Citybus in Belfast – and destroyed there.

Left: It's 27 March 1970 but so far Reigate's MBS 271 has only had its front roundel removed and LONDON TRANSPORT fleetname obliterated. This bus would rack up a fairly respectable eleven years in service, moving on eventually to Windsor.

Left: Desperate vehicle shortages by the mid-1970s obliged London Country to turn to their old progenitor for help, and it came in the form of Merlins that LT didn't want any more but at the present was having trouble selling. After six years at Loughton on the 20 MB 386 still had a year's worth of CoF left and, between October 1975 and November 1976 spent it at Garston. On 14 March 1976 it is seen on the 311 at Shenley.

Above: London Transport amended its ongoing order of Merlin single-deckers to incorporate the shorter chassis, which now assumed the original Swift name. The green ones comprised SMs 101-148 and 449-538, and since they were delivered new to London Country, were registered by the new organisation with the Surrey marks closest to its Reigate headquarters. On 28 August 1973 Swanley's SM 493 enters picturesque Wrotham.

Right: Dunton Green's SM 534 is seen at Chelsham on 20 July 1972. This bus lasted just seven years, being sold in 1978 after service at Windsor.

Right: With the regular supply of vehicles from London Transport cut off (and it hadn't been particularly regular in recent years anyway), London Country had to cast further afield as well as ordering its own new buses. As part of the NBC, it could now draw upon circumstances corporate-wide, and one of those was when a batch of 21 Alexander-bodied AEC Swifts was diverted from South Wales Transport and entered service on Green Line route 725 as the SMA class. This is SMA 11, allocated to Northfleet and seen on 26 August 1972 at Windsor.

Left: When London Country's own Leyland Atlanteans came along, the clock was set ticking on the company's large number of RTs. Ninety Park Royal-bodied examples entered service in 1972 as the AN class, and here at Uxbridge on 16 July of that year is AN 50, new to Garston the day before.

Left: The ANs were to prove successful; without the frills that London Transport demanded of the DMS, they served out the decade and a half demanded of them without complaint. AN 64 was another Garston bus for the 321, and is seen on 24 February 1973 at Uxbridge. The new livery of the time combined traditional Lincoln green with a bright yellow midriff, and it looked most attractive.

Left: The other great success story of London Country was the Leyland National, which in terms of frills was about as basic as you could get. The company ended up taking the largest fleet of these standardised buses in the country, forming the LN, LNC and LNB classes with long wheelbase and the shorter SNC and SNB. The coach versions were not particularly well suited to Green Line work, however, and were eventually replaced by proper coaches. LNC 45 of Reigate is seen at Uxbridge on 29 July 1973.

CHAPTER FIVE

Routemasters

Right: Stonebridge's RM 1021 is seen at Baker Street on 9 May 1970. Reshaping was about to hack away the western half of the 18, curtailing it at Sudbury and turning the roads beyond to a Merlin-operated pair numbered 182 and 186.

Right: The original livery for the 65 BEA Routemasters matched the airline's colours of white and blue with a black relief band. There were no blinds, but the offside panel was illuminated, as seen on NMY 661E at Heathrow on 28 February 1970. The vehicles towed a luggage trailer.

Left: Hounslow's RM 1072 is seen at Heathrow, midway through a route 81 journey, on 28 February 1970, but this group of routes was about to change; 14 April would see the 81 and 81B converted to SM OMO and the 81C withdrawn.

Left: RM 1111 is ready for the off in Hounslow bus station, which abuts its home garage and is part of its structure. The 81B had latterly fallen back from greater days when it had probed all the way to Shepherd's Bush on Sundays, and by 30 March 1970 when this picture was taken, was just a shuttle to Heathrow again. On 18 April it was converted to SM OMO and five months further on still, withdrawn.

Left: On 3 January 1970 Hounslow's RM 1108 heads through Staines on the way to the bridge and, beyond that, Egham. The section beyond the river would gradually be withdrawn and the historic Staines stand replaced by a purpose-built bus station closer to the town centre.

Right: Stonebridge's RM 1174 is seen in Wembley High Road on 1 August 1970. It had come out of overhaul still carrying its original body, though would take on another one when submitted for overhaul again in 1974.

Right: On 4 April 1970 Cricklewood's RM 1142, fresh from a repaint, stands in Victoria bus station, before the roof was put on. At the time, this Routemaster was wearing a lower-numbered body with non-opening front upper-deck windows.

Below: Vauxhall Bridge Road on 4 April 1970 and three of the four buses visible are Routemasters. RM 2029, about to pass RM 1424, still has its full-depth central air intake grille.

Left: 27 March 1970 sees Hounslow's RM 844 at Longford in the last days of Routemaster operation on the 81; this route, probing out of the London border far further west than any other, would be one-manned with SMs on 18 April.

Below: Hendon's RM 2210 plies the 113 down Baker Street through Marylebone on 9 May 1970. Although the outer end of the 113 was suburban and might have responded well to OMO, the central London section was very heavily trafficked and in the event OMO didn't come until 1986.

Above: RML 2696 out of Hanwell is unfortunately carrying a canopy blind in its route number box when espied at Uxbridge station during the heyday of the 207's period with the long variant of the Routemaster.

Above: Fulwell garage on 30 March 1970; we see RMs 1124, 1193 and 1118, with more in the background. Routes 267 and 281 were direct replacements for trolleybus routes 667 and 601, and both survive today, one since shortened and one since lengthened.

Right: BEA NMY 654E and partner storm westwards along the Cromwell Road on 22 May 1971. This was the second of three liveries carried by this popular variant in their decade with the airline.

Left: Alperton's RM 2161 heads past the Wembley complex on 30 April 1971. It was coming due for overhaul, which would ensue the following February.

Left: The 183's Sunday service had been RM-operated since 1966, the rest of the week being the province of RTs. On 24 August 1969 RM 2186 is seen on the 183 in Northwood High Street, turning into Pinner Road. It left Hendon in March 1972, the exchange of identities producing another Aldenham-overhauled Routemaster with that fleet number and outshopping it to Enfield.

Left: Hendon's RM 2207 plies through Northwood Hills on 10 September 1971, another Sunday. At the end of the decade, this stock number would spend a short period as a Shop-Linker.

Above: The craze for all-over advertisements on London buses flared brightly for a few years in the mid-1970s but burned out just as quickly. RM 971 carries its ad for the Yellow Pages down the King's Road on 11 September 1971.

Right: RM 2140 advertised Bertorelli ice cream during 1972, and on 12 December of that year is seen in Oxford Street on the 88.

Left: The RM and RT families continued to hold the fort through the 1970s as the generations meant to succeed them failed in their task. Even so, these routes would lose their steeds in the years after this picture of Fulwell's RM 1086 and Southall's RT 4024 was taken at the Yeading stand on 22 January 1972. The 90B would be converted to OMO on 6 January 1973 and the 232, having already been cut in half, would be withdrawn on 30 November 1974.

Left: On 27 January 1972 Fulwell's RM 1118 leaves the 90B's Yeading stand to head south towards Kew Gardens. The 90B was one-manned with DMSs on 6 January 1973, but RM 1118 stayed put at Fulwell.

Left: The 207A was an add-on to the main 207 that came up from Hayes and Harlington Station, picked up its parent at the Uxbridge Road and took it further into town, but on 15 May 1971 it was withdrawn. Two weeks prior to that date Hanwell's RML 2714 is laying over at Blyth Road, Hayes.

Right: On 25 March 1972 RM 2161 passes Alperton garage, long-time operators of the 83, one of the longest suburban routes on the system but recently cut in half.

Above: Hanwell's RML 2681 has non-underlined LONDON TRANSPORT fleetnames when seen at Hillingdon Heath on 2 June 1972.

Right: Passing the entrance to its home garage on 28 August 1970 is New Cross's RM 1395. The northern half was operated by Tottenham and the route was shared this way until 1986.

Left: On 24 March 1973 Oxford Street plays host to RM 2104 out of Norwood, passing Walworth's RM 1604. The latter is carrying a plain-windowed body from the earliest 250 production stock numbers, as would rotate through the overhaul cycle every so often.

Left: The 33 disappeared for a while, the number being used in East London, but then came back over its previous entirety to serve as the outer, Mortlake-operated end of the 73. On New Year's Day 1973 Mortlake's RM 1567 is seen in Hounslow bus station, carrying not only the rare outlined bullseye but a set of BESI locators; this was an early attempt at computerised route control.

Left: On a gloomy 13 January 1973, RM 1418 is seen in Oxford Street, passing Selfridges.

Above: Gleaming RML 2512 out of Uxbridge garage makes its way eastbound past Southall garage on 19 August 1973; it had just come out of overhaul and would stay until replaced by a DM in 1976.

Right: In the latter days of RT operation on Muswell Hill's 102, weekend operations were far more fluid, with spare RMs giving way to RMLs, then DMs, then RMLs again; at this point (13 August 1978) we see RML 2404 at Golders Green. At the end of 1978 DMs returned on Saturdays and Sundays, as all of Muswell Hill's RMs had gone by then.

Above: From being among the first garages intended to receive Routemasters, Harrow Weald ended up having to wait till 1978 when the 140 was converted from RT. However, Hendon had a Sunday share that used RMs between 1972 and 1976, after which RMLs took over. RM 2207 was overhauled in April 1972 and is seen not long after in Coldharbour Lane, Hayes.

Left: Leyton's RM 265 sets off from Victoria bus station on 22 March 1974. Romania was not the happiest of countries at that point, to say the very least, but it was trying to tout itself as a holiday destination and purchased space on London bus sides.

Right: During 1978 Alperton's RM 2131 heads through Ealing town centre with a fellow 83 punching it up and a DMS, such as had entered service on Cricklewood's 112 in 1976, bringing up the rear.

Right: The unforgettable AEC, builders of so many of London's buses until 1972, was immortalised in the Iron Bridge over the Uxbridge Road at Southall. But in this sector, its last double-deck products were under threat on 26 March 1976; the Hanwell allocation of the 207 already having been converted from RML to DM operation, the Uxbridge fifth, represented here by RML 2661, would follow suit in two days. In the event, the DMs would struggle badly on this and every other busy route on which they were deployed, and RMLs would come back in 1980.

Right: RML 2398 was another of Uxbridge's outgoing Routemasters photographed on the same day but at Southall on a shortworking. Both RMLs 2398 and 2661 would be transferred to Upton Park to convert the 23 from RMs.

Left: RMLs were the best vehicles for the long and extremely busy 207 since the trolleybuses, but in 1976 the route was converted to DM operation with Hanwell and Uxbridge in a 4:1 ratio. As the changeover was commencing, we see RML 2512 about to give way to DM 1227 at Uxbridge. As it turned out, RMLs would return four years later.

Below: On Leap Year Day, 29 February 1976 RML 2512 is seen again, but this time its Fleetline usurper is DM 1230. SMSs 777 and 685 represent the Swift at Uxbridge at this time.

Above: On 23 April 1978 we see RM 1295 and RM 1622 at Golders Green.

Right: Ten days earlier, the inhabitant of the 28's lane at Golders Green is Middle Row's RM 1112.

Right: Hounslow's RM 1911 heads west down Chiswick High Road on 12 July 1979. The 237 had been elevated from a purely Middlesex backwater route to a key trunk route when its remit was swapped with the 117.

This page: All three of these pictures were taken on 31 March 1979, the last day of British Airways' Routemaster-operated service from Gloucester Road to Heathrow Airport. It had been rendered redundant by the coming of the more direct Piccadilly Line extension, but the Routemasters would be much missed. Seen at Gloucester Road Air Terminal in two poses is NMY 658E, and leaving that location, KGJ 619D with badly skew-whiff numberplate.

Right: It is hard to imagine that the glorious Gothic pile that is St Pancras station was slated for demolition in the manner of Euston not far up the road. True, it's dirty in this 8 July 1979 shot that also features Putney's RML 886 on the 14, but that's easily remedied.

Above left: The RCL class of lushly-fitted Green Line coaches reached their end at London Country in 1979 but were bought back by London Transport with a view to using them to replace some of the DM class on busy central London crew work.
The 149 was the route chosen, and the RCLs were phased in between 10 August 1980 and the end of that year, from both Edmonton and Stamford Hill garages.
On 5 December 1980, as night falls over Victoria, RCL 2251 is ready to go.

Above right: RCL 2251 has left and next up is RCL 2250. To ensure the speed of open boarding, the RCLs' platform doors were removed, although the original rears with emergency exit door at the back were retained.

Left: Inside the RCLs, the luxurious seating was retained, although now with DMS-type moquette, as seen on RCL 2239 while it was being readied at Chiswick in May.

Above: How splendid the marvellous Shillibeer livery would have looked had RCL 2221 carried it onto the 149, but this bus never re-entered service, being kept at Chiswick for experimental use. This is where it is seen on 14 April 1980, as the other Shillibeers were generally undergoing repaint back into red.

Right: The last day of Turnham Green garage was 9 May 1980, and to mark the event the staff turned out RM 435 with balloons and streamers. It would not go far, like its fellow inhabitants moving just up the road to the new Stamford Brook garage, formerly Chiswick tram depot.

Left: And here is Stamford Brook garage on 12 May 1980, its third day of operation. Setting off for its home is Stonebridge's RM 728 after stopping off here for unknown reasons, while in the other lane is Metrobus M 138, ready for the off on the small retained allocation on the 267.

Left: On 27 May 1980 RMA 46 is pictured in the dip at Chiswick Works; it was Abbey Wood's staff bus and had held onto its third and final British Airways livery, albeit now with London Transport adverts. The RMAs were numbered in order of acquisition rather than, more logically, to match their registrations.

Below: RM trainers at Chiswick on 14 May 1980. At this point in time, to coincide with the general reprieve of the Routemaster family and drive to return as many of its members to frontline service as possible, the RM trainers started to be readied for service and their place taken by DMSs withdrawn prematurely but with some potential still in them.

CHAPTER SIX

OMO

Right: London Transport's first rear-engined double-deckers were not actually used as OMO vehicles until some time after such operation had been legalised; having had their start on evaluation alongside Routemasters in central London, the XAs were moved to Croydon in 1970, where sleepy route 234 became their pitch. On 20 July 1972, the year before the XAs were sold en bloc to Hong Kong, XA 17 is seen in Wallington.

Below: XA 17 is seen on the same day. The proportion of the XA class not allocated to Croydon after the time in town came to an end went to Peckham for the P3, but all were taken out of service in March 1973 and sold to China Motor Bus.

Left: After successful trials with the specialist Red Arrow route 500 in the West End, London Transport plunged into huge orders for AEC Merlins, reckoning that the sea change that was standee flat-fare OMO would be easily accepted across London. It wasn't, and the Merlins' lack of reliability did not help even though the buses were attractive and clearly of LT lineage in external design. On 18 September 1971 Hanwell's MBS 239 arrives at Greenford on the E2, a new flat-fare route that replaced RT-operated route 97.

Left: MBS 218 was another Hanwell Merlin and is seen a hundred yards down the street about to enter Otter Road to reach Windmill Lane, which served as the stand for a handful of routes terminating at Greenford, but the route was the E1, which combined the outermost end of the 83 and bent it back almost on itself to replace the 211.

Left: Later in the production run of 665 Merlins, Harrow Weald would receive some for the 136, a short route that had been introduced in 1966 with RFs. Only two were needed, and on 23 November 1971 at Middle Road by Roxeth Hill we see MBS 555, which had actually begun at Hounslow but was replaced there by an SMS.

Right: On 23 August 1969 new route A1 began, using four MBSs from Hounslow; it was an express service linking the western limit of the Piccadilly Line at the time (Hounslow West) with Heathrow Airport. MBS 565 is seen at Hounslow West on 25 April 1971.

Right: It was decided to replace Hounslow's MBSs with SMSs, and on 30 January 1971 the Merlins displaced were transferred to Harrow Weald to one-man the 209 (ex-RT). Pinner is the location of MBS 554 once that change had bedded in.

Right: Route 297, introduced in 1968, was converted from RT to MB operation on 21 July 1969, but only on Mondays to Fridays; its Saturday service remained RT-operated. MB 622 was one of eight single-doored Merlins to receive the WMT-G combination of registrations, and is seen at Perivale station on 24 October.

Left: The first fifteen Merlins were bodied by Strachans as the XMS and XMB classes, but when their experimental use on the Red Arrows had ended, were renumbered into the MB class (MB rather than MBS, to reflect their conventional-OMO status, which didn't differentiate between the number of doors) and allocated all over the fleet. XMB 4 thus became XMS 9 and finished as MB 9. It spent the end of 1971 and half of 1972 at Harrow Weald, and on 7 April 1972 has been rostered on the 258. It is seen at Watford Junction, the northwestern extremity of red bus operations.

Left: A peep through the doorway of Alperton garage on 25 March 1972 allows a comparison of the rear ends of Strachan-bodied MB 11 and Metro-Cammell-bodied MB 193.

Below: On 25 October 1969 the 79 and 79A were converted to MB OMO. Alperton's MB 188, seen opposite its home garage, had been new as MBA 188 but was replaced on the Red Arrows by a newer Merlin still.

Right: MBs 304-397 were single-doored, and MBs 331-344 were new to Southall for the 282, which was created on 30 November 1968 out of the outer end of the 232. MB 336 demonstrates in Field End Road on 30 July 1971.

Right: Fellow route 282 newcomer MB 337 is arriving at Northwood station, with its blinds already set for the return journey to Greenford.

Right: MB 341 is in Green Lane at Northwood on 24 August 1969. This bus, like most of its peers, would serve just five years and depart for scrap.

Left: On 14 June 1969 new route H1 was commissioned as a straight renumbering of RLH-operated 230; MBS 502 of Harrow Weald comes into South Harrow station forecourt on 24 July 1971. The 'coin-in-slot' symbols were a shortlived visual reminder to passengers that these were flat-fare buses.

Below: By the time of this 11 February 1976 shot, it would be easy to believe that Merlins and Swifts had completely taken over the workings of Harrow Weald garage; sure, we see MB 629 on the 258, SMS 249 on the 114 and SMS 727 on the 136, but neither Merlins nor Swifts would last the decade out here.

Right: The Merlins may have been vilified by operator, passengers and enthusiasts alike, but there was one place they fit just right, and that was the Red Arrow network. Two rotations of MBA-class stock left a G- and H-reg hard core on the routes which would stay put for a decade, and MBA 602, seen in Oxford Street, was one of them.

Right: By the tail end of Red Arrow MBA operation, the Merlins (and Swifts that had come to join them) had received huge white roundels over their front panels. On 8 December 1980, Victoria's MBA 517 is ready to leave Victoria bus station.

Below: Unlike MBA 517, which had only come to Victoria in 1976, MBA 549 was a Red Arrow lifer and spent a more than adequate eleven years plying the 500 and 507 out of Victoria. It is also seen at Victoria on 8 December 1980.

Left: Night symbolically falls on the Red Arrow Merlins as we see MBA 614, also a lifelong Victoria bus and unusually, the recipient of a late-life overhaul which was intended to keep it going until the replacement order of National 2s arrived in 1981.

Below: MBA 582's Red Arrow career had been spent at Walworth until overhaul in September 1980, after which it was outshopped to Victoria for its final months. Its subsequent use as an ancillary fleet member by London Transport enabled it to last into preservation, one of a very small number of Merlins to do so.

Right: The 838 AEC Swifts were not as distinguishable from the longer Merlins as you might think, as the shorter length remained in proportion; perhaps an easier way of identification of the SM and SMS classes was the addition of an offside foglight to accompany revised legislation. Hounslow garage was a long-time user of Swifts, and on 5 December 1971 we see SMS 723 at Hounslow bus station when new. It was actually delivered for the 116 but here services an earlier conversion.

Right: On 4 December 1971 the 222 at Uxbridge was converted from RT to SMS operation, and on 27 December 1972 SMS 770 is caught leaving West Drayton station. The final 100 SMSs were delivered with wider-spaced headlights, again as a result of legislation which in this case was intended to make buses visible at night to their very edges.

Right: SMS 784 was another Swift new to Uxbridge for the 222, and on Boxing Day 1972 is threading its way through Windsor Street in Uxbridge town centre, about to turn into the High Street.

Left: Allowing comparison between Swift fronts at either end of the production run, we see Harrow Weald's SMS 751 and Edgware's SMS 83 on the approaches to Harrow-on-the-Hill station on 31 March 1973. Much later, the latter bus would have its centre door crudely barred off, extra seats fitted and be reclassified SMD.

Left: SMS 609 spent its whole life (1971-78) at Southall; during that short career it is crossing the bridge over the line at Hayes and Harlington station.

Below: On 19 August 1973 Swifts were well entrenched at Southall, personified by SMSs 320, 253 and 614 beside RTs 4553 and 1257.

Right: A practice stopped only relatively recently was the differentiation of special workings through the use of black-on-yellow blind panels, and that on Harrow Weald's SMS 753 denotes a bifurcation via Bessborough Road between Harrow and South Harrow, where the shot was taken on 30 July 1977. SMS 753 was later detached for publicity use (see facing page).

Above: SMS 231 had seen service at Hornchurch, Leyton and Willesden before coming to Uxbridge in July 1973, and even then its travels would not be over, as it finished out its career at Edgware. It is coming into Ruislip station forecourt.

Right: The E3 in particular had struggled with Merlins due to their 36ft length, and in due course they were replaced by SMSs. On 11 August 1978 Hanwell's SMS 830 is caught on Chiswick High Road attempting to cram itself with that entire queue's worth of apprehensive passengers.

Above and below: Two Swifts became ancillary vehicles for London Transport after their service careers had been brought prematurely to a close; SMS 753 (this picture) was converted at the end of 1978, gaining the code SPB 753 for the cause, while SMD 441 (below) followed in 1981 as a recruitment bus.

Right: This shot of Hounslow's SM 39 in the fuelling line at its home garage on 5 December 1971 shows the original livery on the first fifty Swifts, with outlined roundel, gold fleetnumbers and red fleetname over a grey band and red doors. Substantial changes would ensue, as depicted in the picture below.

Right: Desperate vehicle shortages, particularly of DMSs by the second half of the 1970s, obliged the emergency allocation of Swifts here and there, and the fifty single-doored SMs found themselves sent all over the fleet. SM 18 came to Southall in April 1978, by which time the route number on the blinds fitted to Merlins, Swifts and RFs had been switched to the nearside and the livery altered to turn the grey band white, the red doors yellow and top them off with large filled white roundels. It is in Reservoir Road on 1 April 1979, the day the 273 was extended to Ruislip Lido.

Right: SMS 290 is more what you'd expect on the 273 by the mid-1970s, though is letting the side down somewhat through having allowed its nearside windscreen wiper to flop below the glass. Although the similar equipment on DMSs was replaced by a nearside pantograph wiper upon overhaul, the Swifts were never similarly treated. It is seen on 7 September 1973, in the bend in West End Road just south of Ruislip Station.

Left: The rear of the Merlin and Swift followed the RF class more closely than their ultra-modern status would admit, with the blind box requiring ever such a slight suggestion of a roofbox. However, the printing of a second set of blinds with just a number on proved unintentionally wasteful when passengers continued to clamour for the standards of rear blind box information that had excelled so on the RT and RM families. There isn't any side blind provision at all on SMS 328, and passengers at this West Ruislip spot would have had to run to the front to check the bus was actually going where they wanted.

Left: On 4 December 1971 the 195 was introduced (or rather, re-introduced) but this time was an SMS-operated route from Southall. SMS 619, seen at Blyth Road, Hayes, had been delivered earlier in the year for the 92 but could now add the new route to its quiver. It lasted only the seven years afforded by its Certificate of Fitness and was sold for scrap at the end of 1978.

Left: Sister bus SMS 619, seen at the Hoover factory in Perivale, followed an identical career to its sibling, serving only at Southall and ending up as scrap before the end of 1978.

Right: SMS 741 is one of Harrow Weald's buses when pictured at Ruislip station on the 114; after its initial CoF had run down it was recertified, albeit without a repaint, and saw further use at Hanwell, Thornton Heath and Uxbridge.

Above: SMS 727 served at three garages in its nine years; the first seven years were spent at Harrow Weald, whose 114 it is seen operating at Victoria Road in Ruislip Manor on 25 August 1973. After recertification it passed to Southall and finished its career at Edgware.

Right: The 114 was converted from RT to SMS OMO on 30 October 1971 and SMS 747 was one of the complement into Harrow Weald for the purpose. It spent its whole career here, and is seen at Ruislip Lido.

Left: SMS 75 was new to Edgware in June 1970 for the 142, 186 and 286, and is still in this role at Harrow, Station Approach two years later. In due course it would be the pioneer SMD, which involved adding more seats without taking out the central doorway.

Left: SMS 757 spent all but the last of its seven years in service at Harrow Weald; during that time, it is seen at Ruislip station on the 114.

Left: SMS 666 was an unusually well-travelled Swift; its brief spell at Harrow Weald between April and June 1972 is caught at Ruislip Lido, but in the end it only managed four years at all; perhaps blame its stock number!.

Right: Seen at Uxbridge station on 29 July 1973 is SMS 777, loading up for a journey to Heathrow Airport on the 223. It was a lifelong Uxbridge bus, serving there between 1971 and 1978.

Right: At the Hounslow end of the 222 is Uxbridge's SMS 781; like its counterpart depicted above it served just one Certificate of Fitness, all of it at Uxbridge.

Right: The entirety of SMS 758's licence was served at Harrow Weald; here it is performing a short run from Ruislip Station to the Lido.

Left: SMS 782 turned out to be a lifer at Southall; it was bought for the 195 but is seen here at West Ruislip on the 273, which was added to the garage's SMS roster on 6 January 1973.

Left: It's 26 February 1972 and SMSs 767, 759 and 774 are ready for service on the 222 at Uxbridge, alongside RML 2680, one of the 207's long Routemasters and, further back, RFs for the 224.

Left: SMS 787, seen inside Southall garage on 19 August 1973, is carrying a lazy blind for a shortworking of the 273, and so is SMS 331 farther back. SMS 787 was in service only seven years, but its final six months saw it transferred out of Southall, first to Hanwell and finally to Edgware.

Right: SMS 774 served seven years at Uxbridge; no more, no less. On 27 December 1972 it is seen at its home station, on just another routine 222 journey.

Right: On 30 June 1973 the 223 was converted from RF to SMS operation on Sundays, using buses spare from the 98, and on 19 August SMS 759 is turning from Pembroke Road into Ruislip High Street. It did the usual uninterrupted seven years at Uxbridge that was common to most of this range of stock numbers, but was kept around after delicensing, undergoing a recertification that put it back into service, this time at Harrow Weald, before it was selected to join the Red Arrow fleet and thereby live out a lifespan that made it pay its way rather better than did most of its sisters.

Right: SMS 770 wasn't so lucky; its career was as straightforward as into Uxbridge December 1971, repainted in November 1974, withdrawn in October 1978 and sold for scrap in March 1979.

Above left: The DMS entered service on 2 January 1971 and would balloon to 2,646 examples over the next seven and a half years. Not long after the conversion of the first route, the 220, Shepherd's Bush's DMS 20 and 3 are seen heading southbound along Scrubs Lane.

Above: The sheer number of bodies needed required a second supplier to be sourced, and Metro-Cammell filled in more than adequately. DMS 1365 entered service on 6 January 1973 when Fulwell's 90B was one-manned, and is seen later in the year on stand at Northolt.

Left: Park Royal-bodied DMS 734, seen at Greenford station, was new to Southall in October 1973, but by this time the remit of the DMS had been switched from replacing RTs and Routemasters to clearing out Merlins and Swifts; the 92 had been the province of the latter until 27 October 1973.

Right: For all the noble intentions of the DMS to propagate one-man operation throughout London, 580 of the eventual 2,646-strong class were crew-operated DMs, rushed into production to fill in for RTs falling out from CoF expiry. The 207, by far the strongest route in west London, was treated in two stages during the late winter and early spring of 1976, and DM 1200, seen at Hillingdon on Leap Year Day 1976, was one of fifty deployed to Hanwell.

Right: Hanwell and Uxbridge shared examples of Park Royal- and Metro-Cammell-bodied DMs when the 207 was converted, and DM 1821, in Uxbridge High Street almost at the end of a westbound journey, had been new to Potters Bar in April 1975 but was transferred to Hanwell the following February.

Right: DMS 1557 also began as a crew-operated bus, at Potters Bar for the 134, but was always intended to be an OMO vehicle and, when replaced by a purpose-built DM, was transferred to Southall. It is seen at Greenford Station.

Left: DMS 807 was also a crew bus from the start, and after spending most of 1974 on the 149 out of Edmonton, was converted for OMO at the end of the year and transferred to Hendon in time for the one-manning of the 183 on 4 January 1975. Three years later it is seen laying over at Golders Green.

Below: Then there were the 164 Scania BR111DHs with Metro-Cammell bodywork, collectively known as the Metropolitan and carrying the MD class code. All were crew buses, MDs 1-113 for the 36, 36A, 36B and 63 out of Peckham and MDs 114-164 for New Cross's 53. They performed better than the DMSs but struggled with corrosion problems and were as similarly ill-suited to central London crew operation as were the DMs, so were soon redeployed to south-east London. On 8 July 1979 Peckham's MD 106 sets off from King's Cross.

Above: The M class of MCW Metrobuses would eventually comprise 1,485 members, but the first of them was known as MT 1 for a while before it was decided to simplify the code, irrespective of whether the buses were crew or OMO. In July 1980 M 1 is seen at Chiswick, and today can still be encountered in original condition, courtesy of Ensignbus.

Right: Ms took over Turnham Green's 91 at the tail end of 1979 but would only spend a few months there, as the garage's complement was transferred to nearby Stamford Brook on 10 May 1980. On the previous day, M 152 reposes in Turnham Green's doorway.

Above left: The first 54 Ms wore the attractive 'white-top' livery, combining it with the more unusual black-on-white numberplates in the Serck typeface. M 54 was new to Fulwell and is seen on 13 July 1979 in Turnham Green.

Above: Ms then lost their white relief and resumed the classic London Transport white-on-black numberplate, for which a derogation had been obtained. M 92 started at Southall and in this 14 October 1979 shot has completed one of the 273's Sunday-only journeys to Ruislip Lido.

Left: Turnham Green closed on 10 May 1980 and in its place came Stamford Brook, inheriting the V code and a selection of Routemasters, Metrobuses and LSs. M 136 is seen on 12 May about to head out on the minority allocation on route 267, otherwise the province of Fulwell.

Above: The elegant Titan was the product of greater collaboration between British Leyland and London Transport, and it was hoped that the model would be more reliable than the ill-starred DMS. After some industrial difficulties principally caused by Leyland's closure of Park Royal, where the first 250 were built, production resumed at Workington and LT eventually amassed 1,125 Ts. T 34, seen on 21 July 1979 at Chiswick, would commence at Hornchurch and rack up over 21 years in service.

Right: T 201 was new in April 1980 and is seen at Aldenham on the 24th of that month awaiting allocation, which would be to Barking in July. This Titan only managed twelve years in service, however, and was sold to Merseybus in December 1992.

Above: Six Metro-Scanias were taken in 1973 to evaluate alongside six Leyland Nationals, and although the latter prevailed, MS 2 was kept as a testbed. Pictured at Chiswick on 14 May 1980, it was subsequently sold and is now preserved.

Below: London Transport came late to the Leyland National, but liked them so much that they ended up amassing the second biggest fleet in the country. LS 312 was new to Harrow Weald and is seen on 23 September 1979 in Ruislip.

Above: Another Leyland National new to Harrow Weald was LS 339, new in August and seen at Ruislip Lido on 2 September 1979.

Right: LS 418 made its way to Uxbridge in September 1980 and on 5 October reposes inside its garage alongside fellow Nationals and one of the special-liveried BLs for the 128.

Left: The first five minibus routes quickly outgrew their Ford Transits but still required vehicles small enough to get through the narrow streets they served. The Bristol LHS6L fit this bill, and 17 were ordered, personified on 15 April 1979 by Stockwell's BS 9, blinded for the P4. Larger vehicles still were needed, and the BSs didn't last long.

Left: The BL was the longer version of the LH chassis, and 95 came to London Transport in 1975-76. The last three plus an earlier one drafted in found themselves put to work on the 128, a service from Uxbridge serving seemingly as much of the borough of Hillingdon as it could. On 22 June 1977 BL 95 and partner could be found at Chiswick. Note the offside blind box, a feature not seen since the RTs and never again after this.

Below: The BLs were all delivered in LT's white-top livery of the mid-1970s, but in time lost this for unedifying all-over red. On 24 April 1980 BL 24 is in works for repaint; it had come from Sutton and would return there.

CHAPTER SEVEN

Silver Jubilee

Right: For HM The Queen's Silver Jubilee in 1977 it was decided to paint 25 RMs in silver with a red relief band and run them throughout the year on a spread of services. RM 2 was the testbed for the livery, seen at Chiswick on 19 July 1977 but it didn't re-enter service.

Right: The pure wool carpet inside the 25 SRMs, as they were reclassified for the duration, was particularly elegant. It also had to be hardwearing, for the amount of feet that would be marching up and down over it. This one was inside RM 1894 (SRM 17), which was sponsored by Kosset carpets (although the carpets themselves were actually woven by Thomson Shepherd).

Right: The procession gets under way, and from the platform of RM 1894 (SRM 17) we see RM 1906 (SRM 18) crossing Westminster Bridge. Its two-stage spell in silver would be accomplished first at Bow for the 25 and then at Merton for the 77.

Right: The silver Routemasters inch along the South Bank towards Lambeth Palace.

Right: The convoy has now reached Lambeth Palace; behind RM 1906 (SRM 18) is RM 1871 (SRM 7), destined to carry the SRM livery first to Bow's 25 and then Battersea's 19. As it turned out, RM 1871 survived to be repainted back into silver in 2007 by Timebus!

Left: Having reached Battersea Park, the SRMs were lined up again and here is RM 1894 (SRM 17).

Left: The complete line-up of SRMs at Battersea Park.

Left: Time to leave, and the next six months would see a great variety of SRM appearances as the buses fulfilled two separate phases of deployments. RM 1900 closest to the camera became SRM 22, destined to serve first on Victoria's 137 and then out of Peckham on the 12.

CHAPTER EIGHT

Shoplinker and Shillibeer

Right: Another distinctive Routemaster livery was for Shoplinker, an otherwise ill-starred service pitched directly at shoppers. Sixteen RMs were repainted in red and yellow during 1979, and here is RM 2171 at Chiswick on 7 March, a month before the route commenced.

Below: By 26 March RM 2146 had had adverts applied, though in this case were in-house ones. Shoplinker lasted only until 28 October 1979.

Left: Far better was the Shillibeer scheme, not tied to any particular route and like the Silver Jubilee buses of two years earlier, able to carry the message round every corner of the fleet. Once again RM 2 was the guinea pig, and once again it didn't go back into service; it never would.

Below: It goes without saying how splendid was the Shillibeer livery, using to full aesthetic advantage every curve and line of the Routemaster body. This time there would be three phases of deployment; RM 2160, seen at the Battersea Park open day on 15 April 1979, is plated up for Palmers Green's 29, but it would also be allocated to Walworth (route 12) and Tottenham (route 76).

Above: The full line-up of Shillibeer RMs (there were twelve of them) at Battersea Park, plus their DM counterpart.

Right: Phase one of RM 2142's Shillibeer adventure was carried out at Harrow Weald on the 140; on 31 March 1979 it is seen under the windy canopy of Heathrow Central bus station. It was one of five sponsored by North Thames Gas.

Right: RM 2142 then moved to Hounslow for June, July and August, scheduled for one specific running number on the 237; on Friday 13 July 1979 this was AV8 and it is seen at Turnham Green. For the last three months of its Shillibeer spell it worked out of Mortlake on the 33 and 73.

Left: Just one of the Shillibeers was a non-Routemaster, and it arguably outshone them. DM 2646 was the last of the DMS family, new in August 1978, and spent 1979 in this splendid interpretation of the livery, additionally displaying advertising for contemporary Leyland products. On 15 April 1979 it is blinded for the 16A out of Cricklewood, though during its spell at that garage it stuck to the 16. It also served at Muswell Hill and Brixton, two of the other garages operating B20 DMs.

Below: The offside of DM 2646 at the same Battersea Park location. The bus went back into red and served until 1992, distinguishing itself through seeing out the DMS at Sutton, and a decade later still was acquired by Ensignbus and restored to the full Shillibeer livery for the delectation of enthusiasts (and, occasionally, regular passengers when pressed into service as a strike replacement!)

CHAPTER NINE

Aldenham

Above: The classic overhauling system at Aldenham was a marvel of engineering. Expensive, to be sure, and tailored only to LT's chassisless buses, but it enabled them to last longer than provincial counterparts. This montage of 24 April 1980 shows just another day in the works. B510, the body that had come in on RM 703, is being repanelled alongside RCL 2249, repurchased from London Country and used as a trainer at Brixton.

Right: With bodies and mechanicals all renewed and the reunited halves repainted, three RMs prepare for relicensing and outshopping.

Above and below: The Routemaster was a chassisless construct, the mechanical components being contained on two separate frames held together by the bodywork. The A-frame contained the engine, steering and front suspension and the B-frame the rear suspension and axle. In the picture above, the frames have been 'pinned' together once the body has been dismounted, and below we see the reunited halves after cleaning and silver painting.

Right, below and opposite:
Upon entry into the works the body and underparts were separated for attention separately and the identity they had combined to form re-applied to a combination ready to return to traffic. The first order of business for the dismounted bodies was to place them in the inverter and rotate them to expose their undersides for steam cleaning. This is RML 2452, reclaimed from London Country in February 1980. The green RMLs, RMCs and RCLs bought back retained their original bodies and only in a few cases spread them to stock numbers even within the batches of former green buses, let alone to the rest. There were nine inverters at Aldenham, three of which were dedicated to Routemasters. RML 2452 would be outshopped in red to New Cross in June and go on to serve nearly 25 more years.

Below: The high bay hall was equipped with six overhead cranes that took the dismounted bodies across the building for attention in their own section of the works. The crane, seen lifting an RM body away, was without doubt the most iconic and best-remembered feature of Aldenham works.

Right: Body preparation: this RM and green RML have been lifted to their assigned positions and are now being worked on, with gantries in place to permit attention to each deck.

Below: As well as the two RCLs visible, the RMs in works as of 24 April 1980 were mostly from the 1600s block of stock numbers. The identity of RM 1690 was outshopped to Peckham and RM 1693 to Fulwell, but RM 1666 had been on the works float and its number was not applied to an outgoing overhaul until December. B602, the body seen here wearing RM 1690's bonnet number, went out in May on RM 631, while B1621 (as had come in on RM 1693) left on RM 1714.

Left: The bodies in this line-up have now had all the necessary repanelling carried out, and it is now time to convey them to where they will be remounted on overhauled chassis; this is done using electrically-operated trucks. B602, late of RM 1690, is here being pulled out of the line.

Left: An aside from the regular overhauling of Routemasters to note some other, more modern types being given attention at Aldenham. These types' lack of mechanical compatibility with the works' system forced LT to invest in more diverse and specialised equipment to overhaul them as complete vehicles, which meant they took longer to do and at a less economical cost, which ultimately doomed the works altogether. Next to RM 1678 (complete, now with body B1588 and ready to leave for Mortlake) are an early Leyland National and a Swift undergoing minor repairs.

Left: These three RMs have now been remounted on chassis from elsewhere in the works and they will be driven under their own power to the paint booth.

Right: Miscellaneous repanelling for repaint, and a shot that shows some of the other classes that staged in and out of Aldenham for regular repaints. DMS 1893 has come in from Potters Bar for a fresh coat after four years in service, and would return to the same garage.

Right: The question of what to do with the DMS bedevilled Aldenham from the moment the expiry of the seven-year Certificates of Fitness of the earliest examples started to approach. Although the modern buses were not designed to have the body and chassis (and it was a chassis in this case) separated, they did make an attempt, only for it to cause so much damage to the bodywork that the DMSs were left intact, which meant having to order two new jigs to overhaul the complete vehicles in. Even then, as withdrawals commenced, DMS overhauls were suspended during 1980 and at this point the only Fleetlines in works were for recertifications on three-year tickets; this is one of them.

Right: The repainting process involved three stages; first a pink undercoat was sprayed on, then the coat of red itself and finally a coat of varnish. To save time, each coat went on while the previous one was still wet. RM 127 was in works for an intermediate repaint rather than an overhaul, and after a three-hour ordeal in the drying oven and a set of new transfers, would return whence it came, to Chalk Farm.

Above left: This RM from the 1800s series of stock numbers is being masked for repaint, with old bits of advert doing the duty of masking panels. Note the aerodynamic panels opposite the bonnet lid; it's fibreglass rather than metal.

Above: The drying is over for this Routemaster and the masking is being peeled off.

Left: Two more RMs fresh out of the paint booth; they had been hand-sprayed and are now having their masking removed. Their rubberised indicator 'ears' have been taken off and will be restored after the drying is complete.

Right: Into the bake oven go three RMs; the one bringing up the rear has had its platform doorway sealed off and the grille taken off so that the engine can be masked more closely. Some bits that don't need doing too badly, like the legend above the used tickets bin and the capacity indicators underneath, are being left and will be reapplied over the new coat of paint even if the old transfers bulge through.

Right and below right: Once the whole ensemble is out, it's to all intents and purposes a brand new bus, and as such is still subject to passing the legal requirements of its continuing road licence. This combination has taken on the identity of RM 1700, carrying body B1659, and before its departure for Hackney garage is about to face the tilt test, that most British of indicators as to whether a double-deck bus is fit for the road. The prescribed limit as to how far an unladen bus was allowed to tilt was 28 degrees, but RM 1700 is resisting a massive list of forty degrees!

Left: Just the re-applying of ephemera to follow now, although for these two, just the roundel has been done; as their bonnets and grilles haven't been put back on yet, we are left none the wiser as to which RMs these actually are. In truth, they will take the identity of the licence still valid from whatever came in works the same day as these are scheduled to go out. Swapping identities was a clever way of not having to waste several months of road tax that would otherwise be going unused, but the Department of Transport didn't care for the process and it came to an end at the same time body separation did, leaving the Routemasters still extant at that time permanently wedded to their final bodies.

Below: Ready to go and resplendent, with only the bonnet left to be fastened back on.

CHAPTER TEN

Miscellaneous

Right: After the overtime ban, London Transport turned two outlying services over to independents, who remained active on them for many years. Elms Coaches had the 98B, seen in the form of ex-Thames Valley Bristol LS HBL 88, turning at Ruislip station on 7 June 1969.

Below: RML 2760, the last of the Routemasters, was always better known for its many decades at Upton Park, but between June 1972 and January 1973 it served at Uxbridge. During that summer it lines up at that garage's stabling point with RTs from the 98 and RFs from the 204, 223, 224 and 224B.

Left: The other portal of the old Uxbridge garage sees RML 2760 again, with recently-overhauled partner RML 2293; together they are flanking RT 502, which was only based here briefly during December 1972.

Below left: Uxbridge bus station facing outwards during the early spring of 1976, when DMs had arrived in force to replace the 207's RMLs from both Uxbridge and Hanwell. Also evident are SMSs, RFs (both London Transport and London Country) and a coach in the increasingly prevalent National Express all-over white. To the right is the old staff canteen building.

Below: Southall garage is seen on 19 July 1973; the runout at the time included RTs for the 105 and 120 and SMSs for the 273.

Inset: As the decade came to a close, a garage-building programme was well along that allowed older bases to close; Turnham Green thus gave way to nearby Stamford Brook.

Turnham Green Garage

ENQUIRIES AT BUS GARAGES

Above: London Transport 1457MR was a 10-ton AEC Militant breakdown tender acquired in 1966 from the Royal Air Force. On 17 April 1978 it was on site at Chiswick.

Right: 702B was one of ten articulated mobile canteens intended for use at remote sites; new in 1948, it lasted only a decade before sale to Liverpool Corporation Transport. Acquired in 1974 by Cobham Bus Museum, it is seen on 10 April 1977 as part of the Silver Jubilee display at Battersea Park.

Right: Breakdown tender 830J was fashioned out of former STL 390; on 31 March 1979 it is seen at Chiswick works, not long before its disposal to the London Transport Museum.

Left: Obsolete Fleet's vintage bus service 100 was a fixture of the 1970s, and its jewel in the crown was ST 922, seen on 8 April 1972 crossing Westminster Bridge. This popular veteran would go on to many more years of distinguished use, participating in the send-off of Routemasters in 2005 and, as this book is written, now appearing in Tilling livery.

Below: The BMMO D9 was a front-engined contemporary of the Routemaster, developed in the workshops of Midland Red, which long evinced a design flair all its own. In later years 5043 was acquired by Obsolete Fleet and, as OM 4, repainted in a red not too different from that it had carried when new. It is seen in Hyde Park on 10 April 1977, the day of the Silver Jubilee LT event.

Above: As part of the commemorations of the 150th anniversary since George Shillibeer first hitched up his horses, 8 July 1979 saw the re-creation of this service from London Wall to Paddington, in the form of a parade featuring not only five horse buses, but examples of as many early forms of London bus as could be gathered together. The replica Star Omnibus Company horse bus is pulled by its two steeds past King's Cross at midday of that day.

Right: The horse-bus aspect of 1979 continued when a service was mounted between Baker Street and The Zoo. It ran every 30 minutes with an adult fare of £1. On 27 July one of the conveyances in question is seen at Baker Street.

Left: There is just one survivor of the elegant Chiswick-designed TF class of 34-seat Green Line coaches that lasted from 1937 to 1953; it is TF 77, and is seen outside the drawing office block at Chiswick Works on 14 May 1980.

Left: On 28 August 1979 we see three generations of London bus under the windblown canopy of Victoria bus station; Routemaster RM 1146, Merlin MBA 598 and Fleetline DM 2532. The roof here was repainted within the next decade but eventually removed altogether.

Left: An earlier but much-missed mode of transport in London was the trolleybus. Efficient, silent and clean, their only drawback was in the need to maintain miles of cumbersome overhead, and this was what eventually doomed them to a premature finish. The post-war Q1 class were good for two more decades yet, only they spent them in Spain rather than in London. No 1768, however, was retained by the London Transport Museum and in this picture taken on 24 April 1980 had just received a repaint at Aldenham.

Bibliography

Books
The London Bus Review of … (1973-1980), LOTS 1974-1981
RT: The Story of a London Bus, Ken Blacker, Capital Transport 1980.
Routemaster: vol 1 1954-1969, Ken Blacker, Capital Transport 1991.
Routemaster: vol 2 1970-1989, Ken Blacker, Capital Transport 1992.
RF, Ken Glazier, Capital Transport 1991.
The London Merlin, Ken Russell, Capital Transport 1980.
The London Swifts, Ken Russell, Capital Transport 1985.
London Country, Laurie Akehurst and David Stewart, Capital Transport 1984.
London Country in the 1970s, Steve Fennell, Ian Allan 2003.
Reshaping London's Buses, Barry Arnold & Mike Harris, Capital Transport 1982.
London Transport Buses, Lawrie Bowles, Capital Transport 1977-1980.
London Transport Scrapbook for … (1976-1980), Capital Transport 1977-1981.
Daimler Fleetline, Gavin Booth, Ian Allan 2010.
London Transport in the 1970s, Michael H. C. Baker, Ian Allan 2007.
London Transport 1970-84, Matthew Wharmby, Ian Allan 2013.
The London DMS, Matthew Wharmby, Pen and Sword 2017.

Magazines, Supplements, Articles and Periodicals
The London Bus (TLB), LOTS, monthly
London Bus Magazine (LBM), LOTS, quarterly
TLB Extra, LOTS, for the years 1970-1980
BUSES magazine, Ian Allan, monthly
SUP-44A London Bus Disposals – Where are they Now? March 2008, LOTS 2008.
Fleet History LT9; The Vehicles of London Transport and its Predecessors; Modern Classes (RM Class to date), The PSV Circle 2005.

Websites and Groups
Ian's Bus Stop (www.countrybus.org)
London Bus Routes by Ian Armstrong (www.londonbuses.co.uk)
Bus Lists on the Web (www.buslistsontheweb.co.uk)